KAREN F. WILLIAMS
presents

Lights, Drama, Worship!

Plays, Sketches, & Readings for the Church

KAREN F. WILLIAMS

presents

Lights, Drama, Worship!

Plays, Sketches, & Readings for the Church

2

ZONDERVAN™

GRAND RAPIDS, MICHIGAN 49530 USA

Lights, Drama, Worship! Volume 2
Copyright © 2004 by Karen F. Williams

Requests for information should be addressed to:
Zondervan, *Grand Rapids, Michigan 49530*

Library of Congress Cataloging-in-Publication Data

Williams, Karen F., 1959–
Lights, drama, worship! / Karen F. Williams.—1st ed.
    p. cm.
Includes bibliographical references and index.
    ISBN 0-310-24245-2 (volume 1)—ISBN 0-310-24249-5 (volume 2)—
    ISBN 0-310-24263-0 (volume 3)—ISBN 0-310-24264-9 (volume 4)
    1. Drama in Christian education. 2. Christian drama, American. I. Title.
BV1534.4.W55 2004
246'.72—dc22   2003014726

Interior design by Susan Ambs

Printed in the United States of America

03 04 05 06 07 08 09 / ❖ ML/ 10 9 8 7 6 5 4 3 2 1

To Pastors Horace and Kiwanis Hockett,
dramatists whose lives exemplify
holiness, excellence, and humility

To Director Lawrence James and Living Parables members,
who have taught me the value of drama in excellence

Contents

Who's Who in the Cast 9

Introduction 11

Easter Play 25

Is It Love or Noise? 37

Tongue Twisters 45

Watch What You Hold On To............................59

The Spiritual Bank 69

Topical Index 85

Who's Who in the Cast

The theatre is an art which reposes upon the work of many collaborators. . . . We have been accustomed to think that a work of art is by definition the product of one governing selecting will.

Thornton Wilder

A play requires a cast of people to produce. So it was with the writing of this volume. Numerous persons played leading roles in bringing these plays to the published stage.

The Director— All glory and thanks to God, my Divine Director, for originating this work's vision and providing the wherewithal to complete it.

Manuscript Evaluators— Edna Brown, James Lawrence, and Denise Owens, I am deeply indebted to you for spending extensive time evaluating this volume and offering invaluable guidance, constructive criticism, editorial support, and many kind words of encouragement.

Reviewers— I offer gratitude for my dear colleagues who spent time reviewing one or more plays and providing significant feedback: Gwendolyn Colvin, Darrell and Tracey Edwards, Joan Daniel, Regina Hoosier, Lilly Lester, and Tonya Williams.

Family and Friends— Deep appreciation goes to devoted family members whose constant prayers and inspiring words provided strength for my journey. Thanks to Arnetta Robinson, Ann Williams, and Fred and

JoAnneWilliams, who read portions of this volume. I'm also grateful for the prayers of numerous friends who graciously asked, "How's the writing going?" Angela Denmark and Delores Steele, thanks for being faithful friends who not only read sections of the manuscript but also offered your prayers, insightful words, and were always willing to assist with this writing project every step along the way.

Pastors and Drama Ministry— Pastors Horace and Kiwanis Hockett, thanks for being dramatists whose lives exemplify holiness, excellence, and humility. Pastor Hockett, I'm most appreciative of your reading several plays and offering kind words of support. Also thanks to Director Lawrence James and Living Parables members for your generous support and for providing an avenue for me to present my writings. Special thanks to "Black Women Walking" staged readers Marcie Hockett, Dorothy Dobson, and Carol Wade, and "Tongue Twisters" performers Leslie Poston and Anthony Jones.

The Producers— Many thanks to the outstanding staff at Zondervan. I'm most appreciative of Jim Ruark, my editor, who graciously guided me through each publishing phase and was always available to respond to my questions and concerns. Special thanks to Alicia Mey and the splendid marketing staff for your expertise and creativity.

The Cast and Production Staff— I offer my appreciation to all who purchase this volume and transform this print from page to stage. Thank you kindly, for you are the ones who bring these written expressions to life.

Introduction

What are you looking at me for?
I didn't come to stay.
I just came to say Happy Easter Day!

I remember young children saying this rhyme for Easter programs when I was a child. This amusing speech, normally recited by a child five years old or younger, always received warm smiles and laughter from the congregation, followed by thunderous applause. I too had my share of giving recitations, which was my least favorite thing to do. The Sunday school department gave all the children short speeches, normally a week before the program. So I practiced my speech—consisting of four to eight lines—all week long in front my family. I even asked my siblings to call my name. They would say, "We will now have a speech by Karen Williams." I would smile at the sound of my name, rise with confidence, stand in the middle of the living room floor, and recite with ease.

Soon the big program day arrived, and I had to leave the comfort of my living room. And with that departure, all my confidence left as well. At church I sat in my seat, my heart pounding with fear, waiting to hear my name. Finally I heard an adult voice at the front of the sanctuary announce those dreaded words: "Next we have a speech by Karen Williams." All eyes turned toward me, and at that moment I wanted to disappear. I arose and made the long walk to the front of the altar. Trembling with fear, I recited my speech quickly. As I made my way back to the pew, I heard a welcome sound, the congregation's applause. Before I knew it, I was in the comfort of my seat again, relieved that I had survived the public ordeal. Whew! That was a lot of work for just a few lines. This was my first experience with church drama—or perhaps more aptly, church *trauma*.

While recitations like the "Happy Easter Day" rhyme may not technically qualify as drama, they certainly capture our attention, as all plays do. As I moved from recitations to acting in plays during my teenage years, I noticed how the congregation maintained rapt attention during a play. In my early twenties when I started writing plays for my church drama group, I began to see these performances as a form of ministry. Around that same time my relationship with Christ deepened, and I discovered that plays, even simple sketches, could touch lives in ways that sermons did not. I saw how the audience was able to identify with the characters onstage or relate to the subject. At times people would tell me that a particular play inspired them or made them examine their relationship with God.

A powerful play can both entertain and bring us into God's presence, moving us to worship. Two authors provide definitions of worship that best explain my heart and my purpose in writing these plays. First, James Burton Coffman:

A good description of worship is that of Isaiah 6:1–8, an analysis of which shows that worship is: (1) an awareness of the presence of God, (2) a consciousness of sin and unworthiness on the part of the worshipper, (3) a sense of cleansing and forgiveness, and (4) a response of the soul with reference to doing God's will: "Here am I, send me!"[1]

The other definition comes from Rick Warren:

> Worship is not a *part* of your life; it *is* your life. Worship is not just for church services. . . . Every activity can be transformed into an act of worship when you do it for the praise, glory, and pleasure of God."[2]

Whether you encounter a cleansing and forgiveness, sense God's presence, or say, "Lord, here am I," my hope is that this volume of *Lights, Drama, Worship!* will provide your congregation with a powerful worship experience . . . an experience that transcends the church setting and becomes a lifestyle.

In this volume you will find short, easy-to-perform presentations for groups with little or no drama experience as well as longer, more structured plays for experienced drama ministries. These plays include three styles:

1. Readers theater ("Is It Love or Noise?")
2. Sketches ("Easter Play" and "Watch What You Hold On To")
3. Feature plays ("Tongue Twisters" and "The Spiritual Bank")

I describe each style in Types of Drama in This Volume (pages 14–16). In Production Notes (pages 17–20), I suggest how to stage the plays and also include some production tips. If you desire to learn more about producing church plays, see the list of resources on page 20.

I have found certain steps to be effective in preparing to perform plays. As your drama team rehearses, you may want to follow these recommendations. First, I encourage you to spend time praying together. During your rehearsals, pray for unity and a team spirit within the group. Pray that God will be glorified through your cast and production team. Pray too that the play will inspire the congregation and allow them to experience God's presence. You may also want to set aside time to fast before the performance.

Next, take some time during your first or second rehearsal to talk about the play: What does the play say to you? Why is your character important in this play? What can you learn from your character? Why is the play's theme important? What effect might the play have on the congregation? Does the play reveal any insights about your relationship with God and others? This discussion will help your group understand the play's purpose and theme, allowing them to see the presentation as ministry.

Last, strive for excellence in your presentation. This means placing a premium on doing your best with the resources available to you and striving to present a quality production. Certainly, selecting a cast, arranging rehearsals suitable for everyone's schedule, and directing a play is no easy task. Yet by allowing adequate time for rehearsals, the production becomes manageable. My hope, then, is that when all is said and done—after spending time in prayer and after the long hours of production preparation—your drama team, in addition to your audience, will not only experience the presence of God but also develop a closer relationship with him.

Types of Drama in This Volume

Dramatic Reading and Readers Theater

Although this volume does not include a dramatic reading, a description of this style will be helpful in understanding readers theater. The two styles are quite similar.

A *dramatic reading,* also called an *interpretive reading,* presents one or more persons reading a script with purposeful vocal expression. Normally there are no or limited props and scenery, little or suggestive movement, and no memorization. The readers may use a black folder to hold their scripts or they may place the script on music stands or lecterns. Since the focus is on the words and ideas and not physical action, the readers must articulate their words clearly, precisely, and expressively. Some readings may involve a group, called a chorus, speaking simultaneously.

Speaking in unison is important in these cases. In her book *Praising God through the Lively Arts,* Linda Goens offers helpful advice for group or choral reading:

> In the beginning it is advisable to keep choral readers to a small number. The more people reading in chorus, the harder it is to read in unison and the more difficult for the congregation to understand the words and appreciate the type of reading. Start with three or four readers in chorus, increasing the number later.
>
> There are three major concerns with choral reading that take special practice: beginning together with confidence, pacing, and inflection. The group needs to begin speaking in perfect unison, to pause together at punctuation and other designated points, and to speak with the same inflection (for example, loudly, softly, harshly, tenderly), emphasizing the same words in the same way, and so on.[3]

Readers theater is similar to dramatic reading in that it does not typically require props, scenery, and movement. It too may include group or choral reading. However, readers theater presentations are usually longer and may include characters who move about the stage. Readers can perform by either standing or sitting on stools. They may also perform with or without memorization. When they memorize the script, they have the freedom to include some movement or hand gestures. Using music stands or lecterns to hold scripts is another way to free the readers' hands. If the script is not memorized, readers should be so familiar with their lines that they need only glance at the pages. Leslie Irene Coger and Melvin R. White, in their *Readers Theatre Handbook,* say that the eyes are the most expressive facial feature, helping to depict a character's attitude and communicate the reading's meaning while helping to maintain audience attention:

If the eyes are kept continuously on the page, the readers tend to turn the whole face downward, and as a result their voices are directed toward the floor and are difficult to hear. The readers should therefore keep their eyes as free of the script as possible. This does not mean that they ignore the script; rather, they must grasp the words in a quick glance so that they may use their eyes for expressive purposes.[4]

These techniques can be applied to the readers theater piece in this volume, "Is It Love or Noise?" which is based on 1 Corinthians 13.

Sketches

Sketches have the structure of a play (characters, conflict, resolution) but are much shorter. Since acting is involved, sketches require characters to memorize their lines. Although scenery, props, and costumes may be used, they are normally kept to a minimum; the emphasis is on the message the sketch is conveying to the audience. Sketches can be serious, but more often than not they are humorous and range in performance time from two to twelve minutes. The two sketches in this collection, "Easter Play" and "Watch What You Hold On To," may run slightly longer than twelve minutes.

Feature Play

The *feature play* is the longest dramatic form included here and therefore requires more production time to allow for extensive rehearsals and interpretation of lines, blocking (movement of characters), and stage preparation. This play is intended to be the main presentation for a worship service or program. "Tongue Twisters" and "The Spiritual Bank" are this volume's feature plays.

Production Notes and Tips

What Each Play Contains

Each play contains the following to assist you in production.

Scripture References: Bible passages in the play or Scriptures to support the theme

Theme: The play's topic or subject matter

Summary: A brief description of the play

Characters: The people involved in the play, or a list of actors (sometimes with character descriptions)

Costume Suggestions: Costume descriptions. Not all the plays include descriptions. These are merely suggestions; add costumes if it will present a better production.

Set Design: Scenery that gives the location and environment of the play; also an illustration of the stage layout. Since sanctuaries are not uniform in structure, the entrances and exits as I have indicated in the script may not work for your stage. Adjust the layout so that it works best for your church. The diagram on page 22 shows stage positions.

Props: A list of items used to enhance the set and the characters' actions

Setting: A description of the scene as the play begins (what props and furniture are onstage and where the characters are positioned). Sometimes the setting is a specific place such as a bookstore or a home. When it is not a designated place, I use the words "No particular place defined."

Rehearsal Notes: A place for the director, actors, and backstage persons to write rehearsal dates and other important information relative to the play

Music/Sound Effects: A list of songs, instrumentals, or sounds in the play (not all plays will include music)

Devotional Moment: A further explanation of the sketch, appropriate to be read by the pastor or program director after the performance. Only one presentation ("Easter Play") in this volume concludes with a brief devotional.

Helpful Tips from Other Dramatists

Warm-up Exercises

Exercises to help the actors relax and prepare their vocals for the stage are called warm-up exercises. The following suggestions are from *The Dramatic Arts in Ministry* by Ev Robertson.

1. Stretch muscles by reaching for the ceiling. Reach high several times with each hand stretching as much as possible. Then collapse from the waist and drop hands toward the floor. Hang as relaxed as possible. Repeat the exercise several times.
2. Shake hands rapidly from the wrist.
3. Shake arms from the shoulders.
4. Shake each leg.
5. Move head in a circle one direction and then the other.
6. Stretch facial muscles into grotesque shapes and then relax after each.
7. Combine basic vowel sounds (ah, eh, eee, ai, oh, oo) with explosive consonants and repeat rapidly. Example: bah, bah, bah; beh, beh, beh; bee, bee, bee; bai, bai, bai; boh, boh, boh; boo, boo, boo. Other consonants to use are tah, pah, lah, mah, nah, cah, etc.
8. Repeat nursery rhymes or tongue twisters. Example: "Peter Piper picked a peck of pickled peppers."[5]

Blocking Tips

Blocking is simply the movement of characters onstage. Charles M. Tanner in *Acting on Faith* (volume 1) provides these tips:

> You need movement to keep the play dynamic.

> You want to keep it balanced. (Don't have four characters all walk to the same side of the stage at the same time. Your stage will "sink.")

> Keep your performers open to the audience—eyes and faces visible—not only when they are speaking, but also when they are reacting to others.

> Motivate the movement. People do things for reasons. The characters in the play must move for reasons. The motivations can be mechanical (to get a cup of coffee), emotional (to hide their fear), psychological (they are lying), or intellectual (they are distracting someone).[6]

Rehearsals

Steve Pederson in *Drama Ministry* and Laura Martinez in *Drama for the Dramatically Challenged* offer advice for the director.

Pederson: "Directors need to view rehearsals as top priority. This means that we're prepared, we accomplish our goal, we use time efficiently, and we approach the work with an attitude of enjoyment. We are sensitive to the needs of different actors, we challenge, speak the truth in love, and encourage. It is a tall order. But it's important because the key to a good performance is good rehearsal."[7]

Martinez: "Point out that when an audience laughs, the players need to stay in character (as if the audience were not there) and at the same time try to sense the crescendo of the laughter. Beginning the next line of dialogue just as the laughter begins will cause many, if not most, of the audience to miss it. . . . While waiting for the laughter to die down actors should . . . attempt to keep the scene alive by using gestures and actions appropriate to their characters."[8]

RESOURCES FOR YOUR DRAMA MINISTRY

Linda M. Goens. *Praising God through the Lively Arts*. Nashville: Abingdon, 1999.

John Lewis, Laura Andrews, and Flip Kobler. *The Complete Guide to Church Play Production*. Nashville: Convention Press, 1997.

Laura I. Martinez. *Drama for the Dramatically Challenged: Church Plays Made Easy*. Valley Forge, PA: Judson Press, 2000.

Rory Noland. *The Heart of the Artist*. Grand Rapids: Zondervan, 1999.

Steve Pederson. *Drama Ministry: Practical Help for Making Drama a Vital Part of Your Church*. Grand Rapids: Zondervan, 1999.

NOTES

1. James Burton Coffman, *Commentary on John 4,* Coffman Commentaries on the Old and New Testament (Abilene, TX: Abilene Christian University Press, 1984).

2. Rick Warren, *The Purpose Driven Life* (Grand Rapids: Zondervan, 2002), 66–67.

3. Linda Goens, *Praising God through the Lively Arts* (Nashville: Abingdon, 1999), 35.

4. Leslie Irene Coger and Melvin R. White, *Readers Theatre Handbook: A Dramatic Approach to Literature*, rev. ed. (Glenview, IL: Scott Foresman, 1973), 151.

5. Ev Robertson, *The Dramatic Arts in Ministry* (Nashville: Convention Press, 1989), 48. Used by permission.

6. Charles M. Tanner, *Acting on Faith*, vol. 1 (Nashville: Abingdon, 1994), 9.

7. Steve Pederson, *Drama Ministry* (Grand Rapids: Zondervan, 1999), 146.

8. Laura Martinez, *Drama for the Dramatically Challenged: Church Plays Made Easy* (Valley Forge, PA: Judson Press, 2000), 7.

Stage Positions

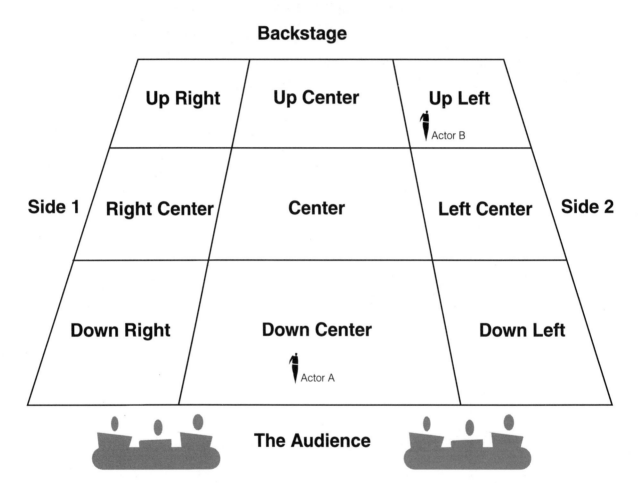

Left and right positions on the stage are designated from the actors' perspective, not the audience's. So if the script states that an actor enters stage right, he will enter from Side 1. Or if he needs to exit stage left, he will exit on Side 2.

Once an actor is onstage, he is standing in a designated position. If he is close to the audience or near the front of the stage, he is said to be in the "down" position or downstage. A position in the middle of the stage is called "center," and positions at the back of the stage are called "up." Actor A is close to the audience and is standing "down center," while Actor B is at the back of the stage and is standing "up left."

Easter Play
(Sketch)

Scripture References: John 17:20–23; Colossians 3:12–14

Themes: Easter, hypocrisy

Summary: Three church members take a trip to their local bookstore to purchase items for their Easter play. When the Bookstore Owner witnesses the dissension that ensues among the members, he concludes that Easter is not about the Resurrection but about material things. The Devotional Moment at the end of this sketch provides a further explanation and helps the audience to focus on the true meaning of Easter.

Characters:

Bookstore Owner: male

Barbara: Sunday school superintendent

Gloria: church member

Michael: church musician

Set Design: A bookstore. Simple or elaborate; a few furnishings to create a bookstore environment.

Props: Two crowns, a box with books inside, a clothes rack with various costumes, and any other props you desire to add

The Stage

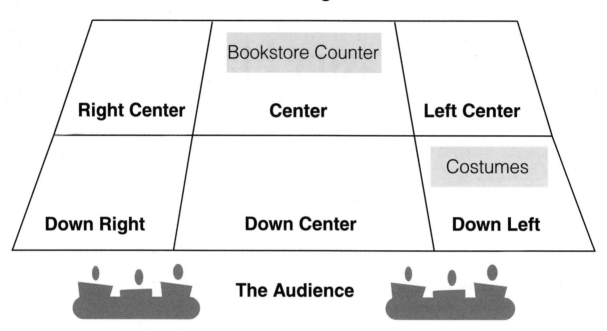

Rehearsal Notes:

Easter Play

Setting:

Bookstore Owner is onstage unpacking a box of books. Barbara enters.

Bookstore Owner

Good afternoon. May I help you with something today?

Barbara

Yes, I called this morning and asked you about two crowns I need for a play. My name is Barbara Lewis.

Bookstore Owner

Oh, yes, Miss Lewis. I remember talking to you. And I have your crowns right here. *(reaches underneath counter)* Here you go. Will these work?

Barbara

(Examines crowns) Yes, these are great. Thank you. They should work just fine. I tell you, I'm so glad you opened your store, and right in time for Easter. Before, I was driving way across town just to go to a Christian bookstore.

Bookstore Owner

Well, I've had other customers tell me this is a good location too.

Barbara

(Looks at crowns proudly) Yes, I really like these. Will you hold these for me? I have more church members coming, and we need to look at your costumes for our Easter play.

Bookstore Owner

Sure. A lot of churches are having plays and pageants. Just take your time, and let me know if I can help.

Barbara

I have some flyers of our Easter play. Could I leave them with you to give to customers?

Bookstore Owner

Sure.

(Barbara hands Bookstore Owner the flyers)

Bookstore Owner

(Reads flyer) "A Resurrection Celebration." *(places flyers on counter)* Interesting.

Barbara

(Excited) It's going to be a wonderful production. I invite you to come.

Bookstore Owner

Thanks for the invitation, but I don't believe in that stuff.

Barbara

That stuff? What stuff? You don't believe in Jesus? God?

Bookstore Owner

(Matter of factly) I believe in God. But the resurrection of Jesus? I don't believe that happened.

Barbara

What? You own a Christian bookstore and sell all these wonderful Bibles and books, and you don't believe Jesus rose from the dead?

Bookstore Owner

Well, I have to make a living. I'm a businessman, you know.

Barbara

So you're just in this for the money?

Bookstore Owner

(Matter-of-factly) Money keeps me in business, and it's certainly what makes the world go 'round. *(politely)* Is there anything else I can do for you, Miss Lewis?

Barbara

Don't you realize that you are playing with Almighty God?

Bookstore Owner

(Thoughtfully) I never thought of it that way. Well, if that's the case, God is a very good playmate.

Barbara

(Shocked) Ah! I can't believe you said that. Well, I'll just put you on my prayer list.

(Michael and Gloria enter. Bookstore Owner ignores Barbara and just shakes his head. He continues taking books out of the box)

Gloria

Hello, Barbara. I hope you haven't been waiting too long.

Barbara

No, not at all. *(self-righteously)* Just here doing God's work. *(looks over at the Bookstore Owner)* Trying to save a lost soul. Let's go look at costumes.

Bookstore Owner

(Speaks as group walks away) Let me know if I can assist. The costumes are on the other side of the hymnals.

Michael

Thank you, sir.

(They walk down left to the costumes)

Gloria

Let me tell you this before I forget. Janice called this morning and said she can't be the narrator because she'll be out of town on Easter. I was so mad at her.

Barbara

What? Why did she wait so late to tell us?

Michael

That's right. The play is just two weeks away. Gloria, why don't you be the narrator? I know you'll do a good—

Gloria

Hold it. I am not being the narrator. You'll just have to find someone else. *(holds up a costume)* How does this look?

Michael

No, that won't work. It looks too plain. Gloria, you would be the best choice. You have a good reading voice, and you've attended all the rehearsals.

Gloria

That's my point exactly. I came to all the rehearsals. Barbara, I told you from the beginning—I'll help out during the rehearsals, but on Easter I am sitting in the congregation. *(strutting)* And I'll be wearing my new designer suit. It's sharp, and I know I'll look good in it. I'm definitely not wearing some Easter play costume.

Barbara

So what are we going to do?

Gloria

I have no idea. That's not my problem. You're the one in charge, Barbara. I help with the play every year, and its not my fault that—

Michael

Forget it! Forget it, Gloria. We'll find somebody. Let's just select costumes, because I have a two o'clock engagement. *(looks at watch)* Hey, why don't you two pick out these costumes. I really need to go.

Barbara

No, Michael, you're the one with the theater background. We need your expertise. It won't take us long.

Michael

(Picks up a costume) Here, this will work great as an angel outfit. *(hands it to Barbara)*

Barbara

Yes, that's good. Oh, this store is great! It's one of the few bookstores that sells costumes. Now let's look at these Roman soldier costumes for the crucifixion scene.

Gloria

(Reminisces) That's going to be a powerful scene with Sister Jones singing "He Bore the Cross." She tears up the church with that song every year.

Barbara

Sis Jones? She's not singing. Michael, didn't you tell Sis Jones at choir rehearsal that we wanted Randy to sing?

Michael

Yes, I did, but she said, and I quote her exact words, "I have been singing that song on Easter for the last three years, and can't nobody stop me"—end of quote. So I just told her to call you because I didn't want to get in the middle of it.

Barbara

Well she didn't call, and she's not singing.

Gloria

Whoa!

Michael

Barbara, I know you're new at the church, so you'd better get ready for a fight on your hands, because Sis Jones has a temper and—

Barbara

And I have a temper too! It's about time somebody set her straight. I'm the Sunday school superintendent, and I have the final say over this program.

Gloria

(Clears throat and speaks in an explanatory manner) Well, *you* don't have the final say—actually, Reverend Sims has the final say.

Michael

Speaking of Reverend Sims, what did he say about my pay increase, Barbara?

Gloria

(Holds up a costume) How does this look, Michael?

Michael

(Examines the costume) That might work. Hold on to it.

Barbara

He said he would let me know, but he didn't sound too favorable. The church budget is so tight right now.

Michael

(Loudly) Well, so is my budget! *(Bookstore Owner looks at them and observes their conversation)* Last year I played the organ and piano for all three choirs, and there were times when I didn't get paid. But did I say anything? No. I didn't make a big deal about it. But I'm not doing that this year. If I don't get that increase I asked for, I'm not playing another key on that piano.

Barbara

You know Reverend Sims will work with you. The church will give you something extra.

Michael

I don't want *something* extra. I specifically need the amount I asked for. If that is not approved by this Sunday, I'm not playing for the Easter program.

Barbara and Gloria

Michael!

Gloria

Now Michael, it would be terrible if you backed out of the play for just a few dollars!

Michael

A few dollars! I have to live just like everybody else.

Gloria

You have to live? You have a full-time job. You shouldn't get paid at all for doing the Lord's work anyway.

Michael

I know you're not talking to me about getting paid.

Barbara

Michael, Gloria! Calm down.

Michael

The church pays you twenty-five dollars for that little egg and flour stuff you throw together and call a cake. Why don't you do that for free?

Barbara

(Embarrassed) Hey, hey! We are a making a scene. People are looking.

(Bookstore Owner continues to look and shakes his head)

Gloria

You know I haven't worked in three months because of the layoff. That's a sorry thing to say.

Michael

Your cakes taste like cornbread anyway.

Barbara

That's it. Let's go outside and settle on what we need to do for the play. Besides, we need to take our business somewhere else anyway. The owner of this store doesn't even believe in the resurrection.

Michael and Barbara

(Point to Bookstore Owner) He doesn't believe in the resurrection?

Michael

Well, why are we here? Let's go to a store with a Christian owner. *(They walk toward the counter)*

Gloria

That's right. *(looks at owner)* Sir, I pray you see the light before it's too late. *(throws hands in the air)* Jesus, keep me near the cross.

Bookstore Owner

Now, why would he do that? So you can crucify someone else?

Barbara

Lord, have mercy. Lord, have mercy on your soul.

Bookstore Owner

Let me make sure I understand. You are leaving my store because I don't believe in the resurrection?

Michael

Sir, we would not have Easter without the resurrection of Jesus. That's what Easter is all about.

Bookstore Owner

Really? You could have fooled me.

Gloria

(Indignantly) And what do you mean by that?

Bookstore Owner

You said that Easter was about wearing designer suits, fighting over who's singing, getting pay raises, and making cornbread cake.

(Michael, Gloria, and Barbara look embarrassed)

Barbara

(Stumbling, at a loss for what to say) No, that's not what . . . You see, Easter is . . . We just had a little disagreement, but Easter is really about Jesus and . . .

Bookstore Owner

(Looks at Barbara) Me? Playing with God? Well, I'm not the only one. *(looks at Gloria, Barbara, and Michael, who look guilty and are speechless)*

(Picks up an Easter play flyer on the counter and looks at it) So is it *really* a resurrection celebration you're having? Or is it just *(emphatically)* Easter *(pause)* play?

(All characters freeze)

Lights Out!

Devotional Moment

Jesus said . . . , "I am the resurrection and the life. He who believes in me will live, even though he dies." John 11:25

"Is it *really* a resurrection celebration? Or is it just Easter play?" That's a question each of us will have to answer for ourselves: Did you come to celebrate Christ? Have you lost the focus of the real meaning of Easter? Is your focus on your new dress or suit?

Has strife between you and someone else in the church caused you to be a poor witness for Christ?

Do you desire to let go of your past and feel the need to start anew?

Easter is not about wearing new designer suits, making more money, or leading a song in the choir. Rather, it is about a humble Savior who gave his life for each of us. Christ came to give us life—everlasting life. And today each of us has the opportunity to have a resurrection celebration by allowing Christ to live in us. In fact, Jesus is the Resurrection: for he not only *gives* new life, but he *is* the new life.

(At this point the pastor could make an altar appeal, inviting those who want to accept Christ as well as Christians who desire to renew their faith.)

Is It Love or Noise?
(Readers theater)

Scripture Reference: 1 Corinthians 13

Theme: Love

Summary: The Readers use 1 Corinthians 13 to show that love should be the basis for all that we do. Without genuine love for God and others, our deeds—though they may appear to be sacred acts of kindness—are meaningless and empty.

Characters:

Reader 1

Reader 2

Reader 3

Reader 4

(Readers may be male or female.)

Costume Suggestions: Readers: uniform colors (example: white shirts or blouses and blue slacks or skirts)

Set Design: No particular place defined. If stools are used, they should be at center stage.

Props: Black folders with scripts (if not memorized)

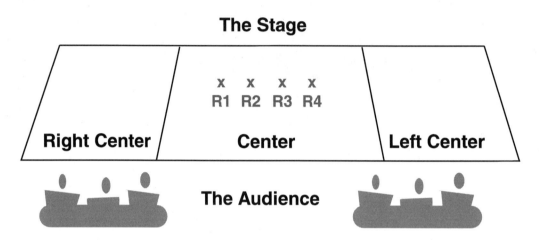

R=Reader

Sound Effect/Music: The "noise" indicated in the script can be made by a musician (or musicians) playing discordant notes on the piano, organ, or another instrument. The later part of this presentation calls for soft instrumental music. A pianist or organist may play, or you may use recorded music.

Rehearsal Notes:

Is It Love or Noise?

Setting:

The Readers are standing onstage or sitting on stools.

Reader 1

If I speak with the tongues of men and angels . . .

Reader 2

(Boastfully) I am articulate in speaking every known language.

Reader 3

(Self-righteously) I speak in tongues and provide the interpretation.

Reader 4

(Pridefully) I speak with the eloquence and authority of an angel.

Reader 1

But if I have not love . . .

All

I'm just empty and void,

And making a whole lot of noise.

(Noise begins but should not drown out the Readers' voices. Readers open and close their left hand, as if imitating someone talking. Their hand movement is in rhythm with each time they say "blah/yada")

Blah, blah, blah, blah, yada, yada, yada.

Reader 2

If I have the gift of prophecy and can fathom all mysteries and all knowledge . . .

Reader 4

(Arrogantly) I am the one endowed with biblical scholarship, academic erudition, interminable sagacity attenuating beyond comprehension.

Reader 3

In other words, (*he) knows *everything* about *everything.*

*(*Use "she" if Reader 4 is female.)*

Reader 2

But if I have not love . . .

All

I'm just empty and void,

And making a whole lot of—

(Noise begins, and Readers perform hand movements as before)

Blah, blah, blah, blah, yada, yada, yada.

Reader 3

Even if I have the kind of faith that can move mountains . . .

Reader 1

Did somebody mention moving mountains? Just talk to me. Why, my faith can move Mount Everest, Mount Sinai, Mount Ararat, the Great Smoky Mountains, and the Rockies in a matter of minutes.

Reader 3

But if I have not love . . .

All

I'm just empty and void,

And making a whole lot of—

(Noise begins, and Readers perform hand movements)

Blah, blah, blah, blah, yada, yada, yada.

Reader 4

If I give all I possess to the poor . . .

Reader 2

(Boastfully) I'm a giver with a capital G. I give to charities worldwide and will give my last dollar just to help someone.

Reader 4

But if I have not love . . .

All

I'm just empty and void,

And—

(Noise begins, and Readers perform hand movements)

Blah, blah, blah, blah, yada, yada, yada.

Reader 1

If I surrender my body to the flames . . .

Reader 3

(Self-righteously) Not many people are willing to suffer as I am. But I'm willing. Yes, I'll be a martyr. I'll stand up for right or a good cause, even if it means being burned to death.

Reader 1

But if I have not love . . .

All

I'm just empty and void—

(Noise begins, and Readers perform hand movements)

Blah, blah, blah, blah, yada, yada, yada.

(Noise continues louder and drowns out the Readers' voices)

Blah, blah, blah, blah, yada, yada, yada. Blah, blah, blah—

Readers 2 and 4

(Forceful) Enough!

(The noise volume lowers)

(Louder) Enough!

(Noise and "yada" stop)

Reader 3

Stop all this noisy living!

Readers 2 and 4

It's causing a disturbance in the church.

Reader 3

Without love there is strife, disunity, and discord in the body of Christ.

Reader 1

And how is our noisy living affecting those who aren't Christians?

Reader 2

Well, if that's what being a Christian is all about, I'd rather stay away from the church.

Readers 3 and 4

Where is your love, my sister?

Readers 1 and 2

Where is your love, my brother?

All

Where is the harmony?

(Soft instrumental music begins to play and continues as Readers speak)

Reader 3

Love is patient.

Love is kind.

It does not envy and malign.

Reader 1

Love does not boast,

Nor is it proud.

It is not rude or very loud.

Reader 4

(Volume lowers slightly)

Love is not self-seeking

Or easily provoked,

And no wrongs does it evoke.

Reader 2

(Volume same as Reader 4)

Love delights not in evil,

But in truth it rejoices,

Always striving to make right choices.

All

Love always protects, always trusts, always hopes, always perseveres.
(Soft music stops)

Reader 3

(Whispers)

Love is not empty and void.

All

(Whisper)

And doesn't make a lot of noise.

Lights Out!

Tongue Twisters
(Feature play)

Scripture References: Genesis 3:4; James 3:5–8

Theme: Power of words

Summary: Words are powerful. We can encourage or harm others by what we say. The Speakers in this play show the destructive path the tongue can take and reveal that only God can help us use words to bring hope, peace, and healing.

Characters:

Speaker 1: male

Speaker 2: female

(Note: Speaker 1 and Speaker 2 will double as Brother Larry and Sister Joyce.)

Costume Suggestions:

Speaker 1: a colorful, Dr. Seuss–style hat; all black (shirt, pants, shoes)

Speaker 2: a colorful scarf, colorful glasses; black slacks or a long skirt, and a bright solid-colored top (gold, purple, red) that matches one of the colors in Speaker 1's hat.

Set Design: The stage is bare except for two chairs positioned center stage. A small table is located to the left of chair 2.

Props: Large children's book with nursery rhymes or stories. Optional: Use spotlights and other lighting (as indicated in the script) to add dramatic effects.

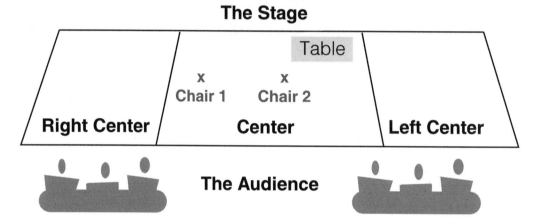

Music/Sound Effects: Music and sound effects should accompany this sketch. The music can be produced by a keyboard. The sound effects include: (1) a door slamming (alternative sound could be a gunshot); (2) blowing wind or tornado. Some keyboards can produce these sound effects.

Rehearsal Notes:

Tongue Twisters

Setting:

Happy music plays as Speaker 1 enters stage right and Speaker 2 enters stage left simultaneously. Speaker 1 wears a colorful hat and is carrying a large storybook. Speaker 2 wears glasses and has a colorful scarf draped around her neck. When they reach the chairs center stage, Speaker 1 motions (in a gentlemanly manner) for Speaker 2 to have a seat. Speaker 2 sits. Then Speaker 1 sits. Music fades. Speaker 1 opens the storybook, and Speaker 2 holds one side of the book. As Speaker 1 and Speaker 2 say the "Betty Botter" tongue twister, they speak in a storyteller's voice, as if telling a story to a group of children.

Speaker 1

Betty Botter had some butter

"But," she said,

Speaker 2

"This butter's bitter.

If I bake this bitter butter,

It would make my batter bitter.

But a bit of better butter—

That would make my batter better."

Speaker 1

So she bought a bit of butter,

Better than her bitter butter,

And she baked it in her batter,

And the batter was not bitter.

Both

So 'twas better Betty Botter

bought a bit of better butter.

Speaker 2

Tongue twisters.

Speaker 1

(Stands) They can be free-spirited frivolity filled with fabulous fun!

(Happy music plays softly, then fades)

Speaker 2

(Stands, takes off glasses, and slips colorful scarf from around her neck as she speaks; her voice changes from a playful to a serious tone, as one giving a warning or caution) But a truly twisted tongue entwined in egocentric energy can emit enormous evil.

(Lights fade to dim. Sinister music plays while Speaker 2 places the scarf on the chair. Speaker 1 removes hat and places it on the table. Both characters' movements are cautious and calculated as they sense that something evil is about to happen)

(To audience)

For the first twisted tongue spewed subtle, sinful statements in the Garden of Eden.

Speaker 1

(Faces audience and speaks seductively and deceptively) "You will not surely die. For God knows that when you eat of it your eyes will be opened, and you will be like God, knowing good and evil."

(Sinister music fades)

Speaker 2

Since the first man and woman succumbed to these wicked words, language lost life and liberty and languished into lewd, lawless lamentations—lamentations walking willfully through the earth wreaking reckless wrath in the world.

(Speaker 1 and Speaker 2 speak argumentatively)

Speaker 1

I hate you!

Speaker 2

I despise you.

Speaker 1

You will never be anything in life.

Speaker 2

I wish you would just drop dead.

(Sound of a door slamming or a gunshot)

Both

Tongue twisters. They dole deep-seated damage to the soul and spirit.

Speaker 1

They are twisted in gruesome gossip.

Speaker 2

Deadly deceit.

Speaker 1

Antagonizing abuse.

Speaker 2

Hideous hatred.

Speaker 1

Venomous vileness.

Speaker 2

Bitter backbiting.

Speaker 1

Malicious mischief.

Speaker 2

Sanctimonious self-righteousness.

Speaker 1

Masterful manipulation.

Speaker 2

Prideful perversion.

Speaker 1

Jeering jealousy.

Speaker 2

Filthy frowardness.

Both

Tongue twisters!

Speaker 2

The tongue is a whole world of iniquity—an unlawful, unruly evil saturated and suffused with deadly poison.

(Sound of a blowing wind or tornado)

These twisters of tornadic proportion freely funnel through homes, churches, and businesses—

Speaker 1

(Wind sound continues)

Unashamedly uprooting families, boldly breaking up marriages.

(Transitional music plays as Speaker 1 and Speaker 2 become Brother Larry and Sister Joyce. They return to their seats and sit. As the music plays, they pretend to be engaged in an enjoyable conversation. Music fades)

Sister Joyce

Thank you for listening to me, Brother Larry. I feel so much better after talking to you.

Brother Larry

Praise God. I'm glad I can help, Sister Joyce.

Sister Joyce

You know, you understand me better than my own husband. I mean, you really listen to me. My husband never listens . . . How can he? He's never home.

Brother Larry

I'll bet he's gone this weekend too, isn't he?

Sister Joyce

Umph. This weekend, and the next two weeks. He's the revival speaker for some church in New York. Then after that he's speaking at a conference somewhere in Los Angeles or San Diego—*(stands and throws up hands in frustration)* I don't know. I can't keep up with his schedule anymore.

Brother Larry

(*Looks at Sister Joyce a few moments, then stands*) Well, Sister Joyce, (*walks toward her*) I have a couple of Scriptures I think will be a blessing to you. Ahh, if you don't have any plans Friday night, I can stop by your house and share them with you.

Sister Joyce

I thought you were celebrating your wife's birthday this Friday.

Brother Larry

(*Unenthusiastic*) Yeah, I'm going to take her out, but I'll have her back home by eight o'clock. (*irritated*) Ever since she had her foot surgery, she just complains all the time—complains, complains, complains. And she doesn't want to be out late at night. So I can be at your place by 8:30, 9:00 at the latest.

(*Sister Joyce doesn't say anything but has an indecisive look; she knows Brother Larry's invitation is wrong*)

Sister Joyce

I . . . don't . . . know . . .

Brother Larry

(*Places his hand on her shoulder*) Sister Joyce, I really feel like the Lord wants me to minister to you this Friday night.

(*Brother Larry and Sister Joyce pause for a few seconds, then face the audience and resume being Speaker 1 and Speaker 2*)

Speakers 1 and 2

(*Facing audience*) Tongue twisters. Oh, the words we use can be deadly.

(Sound of a blowing wind or tornado)

Speaker 1

(Wind continues softly)

Tongue twisters blow through businesses with cold, calculated, corporate corruption, resulting in free-wheeling fraud, elusive embezzlement, and other felonious feats.

Speaker 2

They are not a respecter of persons. Their frightful force is both sinner and saint. They touch down on church members and maim many with malicious rhetoric-creating dangerous disunity.

(Wind fades)

Speaker 1

(Angry tone) I'm the head of this committee. So don't question me; just do what I say.

Speaker 2

(Speaks in a jealous manner) I don't know why they let Darlene lead that song. My voice is much better than hers.

Speaker 1

I heard Sister Alice was—

Speaker 2

I heard Brother Van was at the—

Speaker 1

He said—

Speaker 2

She said—

Speakers 1 and 2

They said!

(Pause)

Tongue twisters. Oh, the words we use can be deadly.

Speaker 2

These twisters carelessly destroy lives, leaving victims painfully powerless in a dark, depressed, degraded state of soul and spirit.

(Light changes to dim or yellow to denote a depressing atmosphere)

Speaker 1

(Somber, sad music plays softly)

They treacherously toss and torrentially turn the soul, leaving behind a timeless, tainted trail of emotional debris.

(Somber music continues to play as Speaker 2 goes to a chair and sits. He looks depressed. Speaker 1 moves stage left. Music fades. Spotlight is on Speaker 2 while Speaker 1 is in the dark)

Speaker 2

(Depressed and suicidal) My life is empty and hopeless. I don't want to live anymore . . . I just don't want to live anymore. *(holds head down in despair)*

(Spotlight shines on Speaker 1)

Speaker 1

My mother was right. I'm nothing but a failure. I never do anything right. I'll never accomplish my goals. I should just give up.

(Somber music plays)

Speakers 1 and 2

(In a depressed tone) The tongue, the tongue, the twisted tongue.

Speaker 2

Who can stop it?

Speaker 1

Who can deliver us?

Speaker 2

Who can straighten these warped, woeful words?

(Somber music continues to play as Speaker 1 and Speaker 2 walk around stage aimlessly, full of despair. Speaker 2 sits in a chair. The spotlights go off Speaker 1 and Speaker 2, and they freeze. The somber music plays softy. Spotlight shines on Speaker 1)

Speaker 1

(Unfreezes, breathes a sigh of despair, and speaks in a hopeless tone) Will my life always be like this—moving from one failure to another? *(shakes head in disappointment)* Granddaddy would always say, "Trust in the Lord; he'll make a way." *(sarcastically)* Well, the Lord never did anything for me. *(sarcasm moves to anger)* You hear that, God? *(shakes fists in the air)* You never did anything for me! I need you to do something for me, God! *(sighs, voice breaks and becomes softer as appealing to God)* Please, God, if you are there . . . help me. I don't want to be a failure the rest of my life. Help me, Lord. Speak to me, Lord.

(Soft music plays as Speaker 1 falls to his knees. Speaker 2 begins to pray quietly for 15 to 20 seconds. His lips move, but no words are spoken out loud. After his prayer his face radiates with peace. As music continues to play, he walks over to Speaker 2—spotlight on 1 and 2— and begins to talk with her about the peace he has received from God. She stands. Music fades)

Speaker 1

(To Speaker 2, with excitement) There is One who can make the crooked places straight. He can season our speech with grace and enable us to speak truth in love.

Speaker 2

Who is this One, and what words does he use?

Speaker 1

Words? He *is* the Word.

Speaker 2

He *is* the Word?

Speaker 1

He is Jesus, the Word of Life and Light. He is the Tongue Untwister. He can say to this twister—

(Sound of wind)

Peace. Be still.

(Wind sound stops)

Speaker 2

"What manner of man is this, that even the wind and the sea obey him?"

Speakers 1 and 2

He is the Word of Life. The Tongue Untwister.

(Soft music plays)

Speaker 1

The Word of Life can untwist the heart, mind, and soul, and give the tongue a whole new language. The Word of Life speaks peace to us.

Speaker 2

Then we can speak peace to our neighbor.

Speaker 1

When the Word of Life speaks hope to us . . .

Speaker 2

Then we can speak hope to our neighbor.

Speaker 1

When the Word of Life speaks love to us . . .

Speaker 2

Then we can speak love to our neighbor.

Speaker 1

When the Word of Life speaks salvation to us . . .

Speaker 2

Then we can speak salvation to our neighbor.

(Pause, music stops)

Speakers 1 and 2

Have you asked the Word of Life to untwist your tongue?

Lights Out!

Watch What You Hold On To
(Sketch)

Scripture Reference: Matthew 6:14–15

Themes: Forgiveness, holding a grudge

Summary: Lynette has been holding on to a grudge against Pam for years. One Sunday morning the pastor preaches on unforgiveness, and the two women have a change of heart.

Characters:

Grudge: male

Lynette: woman with grudge

Pam: church member

Pastor's Voice: an offstage voice

Costume Suggestions: Sunday attire

Set Design: Sunday worship service. Three chairs placed in a row at center stage.

Props: Two Bibles

Music: A musician can play soft altar invitational music during the altar call.

The Stage

Right Center	Center	Left Center
	x Chair 1 x Chair 2 x Chair 3	
Down Right	Altar Down Center	Down Left

 **The Audience**

Rehearsal Notes:

Watch What You Hold On To

Setting:

> *Music (organ or piano) is playing softly. Grudge and Lynette enter stage left. Lynette is holding on to Grudge for dear life. They both have Bibles. They stop and look around searching for a place to sit.*

> **Director's Note:** *It is important that Lynette holds on to Grudge's arm throughout the sketch. The only time she releases his arm is when she shakes him off at the altar.*

Lynette

I told you we were real late. I hate coming to church so late. I don't know if we will be able to find a seat.

Grudge

Don't worry, Lynette. There's an usher coming now. She can help us.

Lynette

(Speaks to imaginary usher) Thank you, usher. *(to Grudge)* There are two seats near the front for us.

Grudge

(To Lynette) No, I'd rather sit in the back. You know I don't like the front row.

Lynette

We have no other choice. Let's go.

(They walk toward the chairs. Lynette sits in chair 2, and Grudge sits in chair 3)

Lynette

Oh good, at least we are here in time for the message.

Pastor's Voice

The title of the message today, church, is "Watch What You Hold On To."

Lynette

All right, Pastor. You preach!

Pastor's Voice

In this life, we hold on to many things. And there are some things we need to hold on to, like when we are walking down a flight of stairs—especially us older folk. We need to hold on to the handrail to keep us from falling. Now holding on to the rail is a good thing.

Grudge

Break it on down, Rev.

Pastor's Voice

And many of us have the good habit of holding on to our shopping receipts, just in case we need to return an item. And that's a good thing too.

Grudge and Lynette

Amen!

Pastor's Voice

Well, church, some of you have gone through many a trial and tribulation—

Lynette

Uh-hmmm.

Pastor's Voice

There were times when you were so down and depressed that all you could do was cry yourself to sleep.

Grudge

(Stands with Lynette holding on to his arm) Yes! *(sits)*

Lynette

You'd better preach!

Pastor's Voice

Even Christian folk were spreading lies on you and mistreating you.

(Lynette and Grudge stand; Grudge waves a white handkerchief)

Lynette

Say that!

Pastor's Voice

Your son is rebellious; your husband is in jail; your wife is going crazy on you. But in the midst of it all, you're still holding on to your faith. And that's a good thing.

Lynette

Good thing, Pastor.

Pastor's Voice

But, my Christian friends, we need to watch what we hold on to.

Grudge

Watch out now!

Pastor's Voice

There are some things that we need to release because they're killing us. I'm here to tell you there are some things we need to let go.

Lynette

Amen!

Pastor's Voice

Church, many of us are holding on to a grudge.

(Lynette and Grudge look at each other, surprised)

Pastor's Voice

You are walking around carrying unforgiveness in your heart, and God is not pleased.

(The voice fades out as Lynette and Grudge begin to talk)

Grudge

Now Pastor isn't talking about you. This part of the message must be for somebody else. You know you can't forget what Pam did to you, or else she might do it again. Now you've been holding on to me all these years, and all I've done is support you, right?

Lynette

Grudge, you're exactly right. I mean, what Pam did to me was awful.

Grudge

She doesn't deserve to be forgiven.

Lynette

Right again.

(Pam enters stage left and looks for a seat. She sees the empty seat beside Lynette and sits in chair 1)

Pam

(Smiles and extends her hand to shake Lynette's; whispers) Hi, Lynette.

(Grudge and Lynette give her a mean look. Lynette does not extend her hand but only rolls her eyes and looks away)

Lynette

Grudge, I can't believe Miss Pam herself is sitting beside me.

Grudge

You did the right thing by not speaking to her. You can't let her ever forget how she hurt you seven years ago.

(The Pastor's Voice now comes up full volume)

Pastor's Voice

Saints, Matthew 6:14–15 tells us, "For if you forgive men when they sin against you, your heavenly Father will also forgive you. But if you do not forgive men their sins, your Father will not forgive your sins." God cannot make it any clearer than this. When you do not forgive others, your own soul is in bondage because you are carrying a weight that wasn't meant for you to carry. *(Pastor's Voice volume lowers)*

Grudge

Lynette, let's go. You don't need to hear this. Besides, you have to hurry up and get home and finish preparing dinner for your guests.

Lynette

I don't know . . . I think I need to hear this.

Pastor's Voice

There are several of you today whom God wants to set free. You don't have to let the devil control your mind and life by holding on to a grudge.

Grudge

(Pulls her arm) Let's get out of here.

Lynette

(Pulls Grudge's arm) No, let's just listen for a minute.

Pastor's Voice

Why don't you come to the altar today and let God do a new work in your life?

(Lynette holds her head down)

Pastor's Voice

(Soft music begins to play) Whoever you are, if you have been bound by a grudge, come! Come and receive the deliverance and mercy you need.

Lynette

(Takes a tissue to wipe her eye) He's talking to me, Grudge. I need to go down there.

Grudge

No! You can't do that. You just taught on forgiveness in Sunday school, now didn't you? So how would that look if you went to the altar for unforgiveness? What would people think? Just hold on to me, and let's find the nearest exit.

Lynette

(Stands and Grudge stands with her) I don't want to hold on to you anymore. I'm tired of having unforgiveness in my heart toward Pam.

(Lynette and Grudge walk down the center to the altar. She is holding on to Grudge and struggling with him all the way to the altar. He's pulling one way and she the other. The soft invitational music continues. At the altar Lynette has one hand raised, and she is holding on to Grudge with the other arm)

(Pleading) Jesus, deliver me from this grudge against Pam. I don't want to hold on to it any longer. I forgive Pam for what she did to me. Please help me forgive her.

Pam

(Looks at Lynette in disdain) Look at her up there pretending like she's being delivered. I forgave her a long time ago, but she didn't even speak to me. She's being delivered all right.

Pastor's Voice

Lord, set your people free in the name of Jesus. Bring healing to their hearts and let them walk in forgiveness. Lord, reconcile marriages, bring unity among family members, and restore friendships.

The Lord is setting you free right now. Just let him have his way.

(Lynette begins to shake Grudge's arm forcefully, and she lets him go. He is thrown across to the left side of the altar. Music continues to play)

Lynette

(Praising God) Thank you, Jesus, for setting me free. Thank you, Jesus.

(Lynette continues to stand at the altar and quietly offer thanks to God. Grudge is still on the floor trying to get himself together. He stands up, shakes his head, and wipes his forehead, trying to collect himself. He brushes off his suit and stands there for a few seconds looking at Lynette praising God. His look is one of revenge and anger. Then a wicked smile appears on his face, and he acts as though he has just received a wonderful idea. He looks at Pam. Pam is not looking at him. He slyly walks over to her and smiles. He extends his arm to her. She shakes her head and motions for him to leave)

Grudge

(Slyly) Listen, Pam. You really need to hold on to me. *(looks at Lynette accusingly)* You see Miss Lynette at that altar? I know you don't think she's for real, now do you. We both know that as soon as she gets back to her seat, she's still not going to speak to you.

Pam

(Thinks for a few seconds) You're probably right, Grudge. If she's not going to forgive me, why should I forgive her? *(She thinks for a few more seconds, and Grudge extends his hand again. This time she grabs his hand, and they lock arms)*

Grudge

That's right, you hold on to me, Pam. I'll take good care of you. Now let's get out of here.

(They proceed to the door and are almost out of sight)

Pastor's Voice

(Offstage) I believe there are others who need to come to this altar. *(Pam stops suddenly when she hears the Pastor's voice)* For many of you, God set you free from unforgiveness, but an old grudge is trying to come back into your life. *(Pam and Grudge begin to struggle as Pam moves toward the altar and Grudge tries to pull her back)* Don't let the devil fool you. The only thing a grudge will do for you is keep you in bondage. Come to the altar and let Jesus set you free.

(Music plays. Pam and Grudge are still struggling, but she overpowers him and goes to the altar. There she stands beside Lynette as Grudge continues to hold on to Pam's arm. Pam raises that arm as high as she can in surrender to God. Pam then reaches out and holds Lynette's hand. At that moment Grudge is thrown to the other side of the altar. Pam and Lynette hug. Music fades)

Lights Out!

The Spiritual Bank

(Feature play)

Scripture Reference: Matthew 7:21–23

Theme: Hypocrisy

Summary: Mr. Davis is a devout church worker who goes to First United Spiritual Bank to discuss his account with the bank officer. He discovers that his spiritual account is at an all-time low—a balance of zero. Mr. Davis has been depending on his church work alone to keep him in good standing with God. This humorous sketch shows the importance of having an intimate relationship with Jesus Christ rather than trusting church work and good deeds to save us.

Characters:

Mrs. Anderson

Mr. Davis

Customer Service Representative

Security Officer

Set Design: A bank environment—simple or elaborate. The Customer Service Representative desk is right center. Mrs. Anderson's desk is center stage, and the Security Officer's chair is upstage left. Two chairs are located downstage left facing each other. One chair is an elaborate executive chair, and the other is a standard office chair.

Props: Two telephones and desktop supplies (papers, folders, and pens) to represent an office environment.

Sound Effect: Telephone ringing

The Stage

		x Security Office
Up Right	**Up Center**	**Up Left**
Customer Service Representative	Ms. Anderson's Office	
Right Center	**Center**	**Left Center**
		0 **Standard Chair** 0 **Executive Chair**
Down Right	**Down Center**	**Down Left**

   **The Audience**

Rehearsal Notes:

The Spiritual Bank
(Feature play)

Setting:

The Customer Service Representative and Mrs. Anderson are sitting at their desks.

The Security Officer is reading a book. Mr. Davis enters dressed in a business suit. He is carrying a briefcase and has a folder in his hand. He walks to the Customer Service Representative's desk.

Mrs. Anderson

(Phone rings) Mrs. Anderson speaking.

Customer Service Representative

Mrs. Anderson, your 4:30 appointment is here.

Mrs. Anderson

Okay. Send him in.

Customer Service Representative

(To Mr. Davis) Mrs. Anderson's office is the second one on the left.

Mr. Davis

Thank you. *(Mr. Davis enters Mrs. Anderson's office)*

Mrs. Anderson

Hello, Mr. Davis, how are you?

Mr. Davis

Oh, I'm a blessed man, Mrs. Anderson. I serve a mighty good God.

Mrs. Anderson

Glad to hear it. Have a seat.

Mr. Davis

Yes indeed, I've been attending the men's conference with Prophet Henderson all week. We've had a rich time. *(looks at watch)* Well, I hope this won't take long.

Mrs. Anderson

So, Mr. Davis, I understand that you are here to discuss your spiritual account.

Mr. Davis

(Pulls statement out of folder) When I opened my statement for this month and saw that balance, I just had to laugh. My account? A zero balance? *(laughs)* Oh, that's funny. So just tell me quickly what the accounting glitch is, Mrs. Anderson. Did you hire a new teller who doesn't know the system? Or is there a problem with new software you're using? Or maybe you just printed out someone else's account. *(laughs)* What happened?

Mrs. Anderson

I'm glad you came in today, Mr. Davis. There is no computer error. Your spiritual account balance really is zero.

Mr. Davis

(Laughs nervously) I don't have time for games. *(looks at watch)* I have another appointment before I attend the revival tonight. Just rectify this accounting error so I can be on my way.

Mrs. Anderson

I would love to give you a better report, but I can't. You have nothing in your account. Now, what you need to do is meet with the president immediately and—

Mr. Davis

(Upset) Hold it. I have been making daily deposits in my spiritual account for the past fifteen years. There is no way that I can have a zero balance. That's ludicrous! *(pulls out passbook)* Now, I have my passbook right here, and I keep good records. Pull up my account on your computer, and see it for yourself.

Mrs. Anderson

I have a printed report right here.

Mr. Davis

Okay. Let me hear it. You can't tell me that all the work I've done for God would give me a zero balance.

Mrs. Anderson

This report reflects your account for the past fifteen years. I'll start with church attendance.

Mr. Davis

Good. I got it right here.

Mrs. Anderson

You have attended 750 Sunday morning church services.

Mr. Davis

752.

Mrs. Anderson

This report does not include this month, but you are right—it would be 752. And your total for night services is . . .

Mrs. Anderson and Mr. Davis

675.

Mr. Davis

Good, good. We're right on target. You can see I am in church every Sunday. I did miss Sunday service a few times in the past fifteen years, but you should also show that for five years straight I didn't miss a single Sunday. Those were the years from—

Mrs. Anderson

Yes, I have it recorded here, Mr. Davis. The next listing is special programs. This includes church anniversaries, Men's Day, Women's Day, Youth Day, and so forth. Your total is 237.

Mr. Davis

Bingo. That's it. What about revivals, conferences?

Mrs. Anderson

I'll get to that in a minute. Bible study attendance—the total is—

Mr. Davis

763.

Mrs. Anderson

Correct. Now your praise report here lists the number of times you praised God—that is 9,023.

Mr. Davis

And if you included this month, it would be 9,139. Nobody can beat me in giving God praise. He's worthy of all the praise. Now isn't that right, Mrs. Anderson?

Mrs. Anderson

Yes, we serve a good God.

Mr. Davis

(Joyfully) Umph, I'm getting happy right now just thinking about his goodness. *(trying to contain himself)* But let's go on because, Lord have mercy, I do feel like praising him! Praise the Lord! *(calmly)* So what's the balance so far?

Mrs. Anderson

I'll give you the balance at the end of the report. Next, we have revivals.

Mr. Davis

(Enthusiastic) Yes, my revivals report alone could make my account overflow. I have attended . . . well, excuse me, Mrs. Anderson. I'm getting excited. I'll just let you tell me the number.

Mrs. Anderson

Along with revivals, I have included your conference and workshop attendance. The total is 749. I see that you've been a guest speaker for numerous marriage conferences.

Mr. Davis

Oh, I believe in saving marriages. There are just too many Christians divorcing these days, and it just doesn't make sense. You should have recorded 103 marriage conferences and workshops.

Mrs. Anderson

You are exactly right.

Mr. Davis

And do I need to mention the number of times I've prayed for people and cast out demons?

Mrs. Anderson

Your exorcisms? Let's see . . . you have cast out a total of 5,219 demons.

Mr. Davis

Yes, I have. And if you include this month, you can add six more to that. Just last Sunday, I had to cast some lust demons out of a sister.

Mrs. Anderson

Next, I have listed the total number of Christian books and other resources you own.

Mr. Davis

(Looks at watch) I tell you what, Mrs. Anderson. You don't have to finish my spiritual account report. It looks like our numbers are the same. I just wanted you to see how ridiculous it would be for my account to have a balance of zero. I mean, with all that I have done for the kingdom of God, my account must be five million by now.

Mrs. Anderson

Mr. Davis, let me explain—

Mr. Davis

(Confidently) Just rectify this account and bring my balance up to the five million or more that it should be. I have a 5:30 appointment, and I don't want to be late.

(Mrs. Anderson shakes her head and is quiet)

Mr. Davis

Well?

Mrs. Anderson

Mr. Davis, you are correct when you say you have done a lot of church work, but in order to apply your works to your account, you must be living the life of a Christian as well.

Mr. Davis

(Outraged) What? Are you accusing me of being a hypocrite? *(stands and increases his volume)* Don't you know the Word of God says, "Touch not my anointed, and do my prophet no harm"? *(Security walks to Mrs. Anderson's desk)* I have been serving God for—

Security

Sir, we do not permit this type of outburst at First United Spiritual Bank. So you'd best control yourself, or I'll have to force you to leave the premises. Do I need to escort him out, Mrs. Anderson?

Mrs. Anderson

No, that's okay. I have things under control.
(Mr. Davis sits reluctantly)

Mrs. Anderson

Listen to me carefully. We do keep a record of all your spiritual activities, because that's our job here at First United Spiritual Bank. But we cannot record any deposits unless they are approved by the President and follow his guidelines. So it really doesn't matter how many times you go to church or revivals, cast out demons, or shout. What matters is the condition of your heart and your relationship with Jesus Christ.

Mr. Davis

(Angry but composed) This is a nightmare. An absolute nightmare!

Mrs. Anderson

Mr. Davis, why didn't you come in earlier? Your account has had a zero balance for the last fourteen years.

Mr. Davis

(Shocked) What?

Mrs. Anderson

Yes. The President applied a grace period to your account yearly. Otherwise, your account would be closed by now. Why did you wait so long?

Mr. Davis

(Takes a deep breath) I was doing great. Every month when I received my statement the interest was accruing, my checking and savings were increasing. So after my first year, I just stopped looking at my monthly statements.

Mrs. Anderson

Mr. Davis, are you saying you have not checked your spiritual account in the last fourteen years?

Mr. Davis

No, I haven't. And I would not have checked it this month, but my wife has been nagging me about checking it. So to get her off my back, I decided to open my statement that came last week. I was shocked to see that balance.

Mrs. Anderson

No wonder your account is in such bad shape. We have tried everything to contact you—e-mails and even double statements. *(shows him a report)* Look, I have recorded here the numerous times the President tried to call you, but either you did not answer or he got a busy signal. So now—after fourteen years of consistent service charges, withdrawals, and overdrafts on your spiritual account—fourteen years straight—Mr. Davis, you are on the verge of filing Chapter 7.

Mr. Davis

No, not Chapter 7!

Mrs. Anderson

Yes, Chapter 7, as in Matthew, chapter 7, verses 21–23.

Mr. Davis

(Nervously) Well, just add my name to my wife's account. We'll have a joint account.

Mrs. Anderson

I'm sure you are aware of our banking rules. Joint accounts are not permitted here.

Mr. Davis

(Agitated and nervous) Well, that rule doesn't make sense. Besides, I was the one who told her about this bank. If it were not for me, my wife's account would be zero too! What is my wife's balance anyway? Her name is Margaret. What's her balance?

Mrs. Anderson

Mr. Davis, you know it is against the President's policy to reveal another customer's balance.

Mr. Davis

But she's my wife. She signed the permit form giving me a right to review her status.

Mrs. Anderson

Oh, I can give you her status but not her balance. *(looks at computer)* You say her name is Margaret?

Mr. Davis

Margaret C. Davis.

Mrs. Anderson

It looks like she has a very high rating.

Mr. Davis

That makes no sense. I'm on the verge of filing Matthew Chapter 7, and my wife—who rarely goes to Bible study—has a high rating? I'm the one who's always telling her we need to fast and pray. I'm the one who's always attending conferences trying to keep our home spiritually stable, while she's out romping around at the kids' dance recitals, softball practices, or tutoring sessions. And you expect me to sit here and file Matthew Chapter 7:21–23?

Mrs. Anderson

I didn't tell you to file Chapter 7. I simply said that will happen if you do not change. What I highly recommend is that you meet with the President immediately and talk with him about your situation. His office is—

Mr. Davis

(Looks at watch) You have kept me here long enough. I'll make an appointment next week. *(stands)* Like I said, I have another important appointment before going to the revival. *(prepares to leave)*

Mrs. Anderson

The choice is yours, Mr. Davis. But I do have one question.

Mr. Davis

(Impatiently) And what might that be?

Mrs. Anderson

Is she worth it? Is she going to make a deposit or a withdrawal from your spiritual account?

Mr. Davis

(Nervously) What are you talking about?

Mrs. Anderson

Your 5:30 appointment.

(Mr. Davis is surprised and speechless)

So, how many demons are you planning to cast out of that young lady when you meet her in that hotel room? Or . . . perhaps you're bringing a few demons with you.

Mr. Davis

(With indignation) I will not stand here and listen to you degrade a man of God. *(walks off and exits stage right)*

Mrs. Anderson

(Calling to him) Mr. Davis! Mr. Davis! I would hate to see you file Matthew Chapter 7:21–23. *(throws up her hands)*

(Phone rings and Mrs. Anderson answers)

Customer Service Representative

Mrs. Anderson, I'm just calling to remind you of your six o'clock board meeting tonight.

Mrs. Anderson

Oh, yes. I had forgotten about that. I'm going to grab a bite to eat. I need a break. Thanks. *(exits stage right)*

(Mr. Davis returns with a look of remorse)

Customer Service Representative

Mr. Davis, Mrs. Anderson just left. Did you need to see her again?

Mr. Davis

(Soberly) No . . . I want to make an appointment with the President. It's concerning my account.

Customer Service Representative

Sure. You can meet with him right now if you'd like.

Mr. Davis

Right now?

Customer Service Representative

Certainly. He has an open-door policy. His office is the third door on the right.

(Mr. Davis hesitates)

The President is waiting for you, Mr. Davis. Please . . . go on in.

(Mr. Davis walks past Mrs. Anderson's office and into the President's office, located down left. He stands between the two office chairs. He looks at his watch and ponders for a few seconds.)

Mr. Davis

(Says a hurried, insincere prayer) God, forgive me of all my sins. You know I had no idea my balance was zero. But thank you for being a forgiving God. *(smiles and speaks with confidence)* Your Word says as far as the east is from the west so far have you removed my sins from me. So, Lord, I know I'm now cleaned through your blood, and I love you with all my heart. Amen. *(straightens his jacket and tie in a self-assured manner)* Praise God for his goodness and mercy. *(starts to leave)*

Voice of God

John Davis. *(the voice startles Mr. Davis and he stops)* Your prayer is not acceptable to me. You have confessed, but you have not repented.

Mr. Davis

(Anxiously) But, Lord, I . . . I just repented. I asked you to forgive me. Your Word says that if we confess our sins, you are faithful and just to forgive us and to cleanse us from all unrighteousness.

Voice of God

You have only uttered words, but your heart is far from righteousness. Repentance means to stop your sin, turn away from it, and go in a new direction. But you are still on your way to the hotel. Room 329.

(Mr. Davis looks around the room with guilt)

I am coming back soon, John. Much sooner than you think. But I am not coming back for those who are playing church. I am not coming back for the lukewarm pretenders. And as for those who file Matthew Chapter 7:21–23, where do you think they will stand? You are familiar with Chapter 7. Tell me John, what does it say?

Mr. Davis

(Fidgety and nervous) Ah . . . ah it says, "Not everyone who says to me, 'Lord, Lord,' will enter the kingdom of heaven—"

Voice of God

(Prompting) And—go on—

Mr. Davis

Many will say, "Lord, Lord, did we not prophesy in your name, and in your name cast out demons, and in your name do many wonderful works?"

Voice of God

And then I will say to them, "I never knew you: depart from me, you who work iniquity." So, John, choose now whom you will serve. Are you going to walk out that door to serve your own desires? Or will you meet with me, not tomorrow but right now, this very minute, to repent and commit your life to serving me . . . in spirit and in truth? Will you get your spiritual account in order? The choice is yours, John Davis. The choice is yours.

(Mr. Davis stands in deep thought for a few seconds and takes a few steps toward the door as if he is leaving. He stops and turns around with a remorseful expression. He walks over to the standard office chair and sits. His countenance is filled with repentance. He then closes his eyes and raises both hands in surrender to God)

Lights Out!

Topical Index
Volumes 1–4

Appreciating Your Gifts
> The Gift Shop (Vol. 1)

Black History
> Black Women Walking (Vol. 1)
> Booker T. Washington and W. E. B. Du Bois (Vol. 4)

Christmas
> All Things Are Possible with God (Vol. 4)
> The Christmas Story (Vol. 3)

Coveting Spiritual Gifts
> The Gift Shop (Vol. 1)

Easter
> Easter Play (Vol. 2)
> Two Gardens (Vol. 4)
> Were You There? (Vol. 1)

Faith
> Don't Give Up (Vol. 4)

The Fall (Adam and Eve)
> Two Gardens (Vol. 4)

Forgiveness
The Curator (Vol. 3)
Watch What You Hold On To (Vol. 2)

God's Provision
God's Provision (Vol. 1)

Handling Failures
The Curator (Vol. 3)

Hope
Don't Give Up (Vol. 4)

Hypocrisy
Easter Play (Vol. 2)
How Is Your Quiet Time? (Vol. 1)
The Spiritual Bank (Vol. 2)

Judging Others
How Is Your Quiet Time? (Vol. 1)

Love
Is It Love or Noise? (Vol. 2)

Male/Female Relationships
The Husband Center (Vol. 3)

Mother's Day
A Mother's Love (Vol. 3)

People Pleasers
What People Think (Vol. 3)

Persistence
Don't Give Up (Vol. 4)

Power of Words
Tongue Twisters (Vol. 2)

Salvation/Redemption

The Curator (Vol. 3)

Two Gardens (Vol. 4)

Single Women

The Husband Center (Vol. 3)

Sunday School

Come to Sunday School (Vol. 4)

Vain Worship and Works

The Spiritual Bank (Vol. 2)

Women

Black Women Walking (Vol. 1)